# Sponsor's Foreword

Goldman Sachs is delighted to sponsor the fifteenth annual Serpentine Pavilion designed by selgascano. As a leading financial services firm, we place enormous value on innovation and creativity. The Pavilion commission is synonymous with these values and we are extremely proud to be lending our support to bring this year's unique and exciting design to life.

London is one of the world's leading cultural centres and we believe that projects like the Serpentine Pavilion encourage the exchange of ideas and perspectives and lead to the development of a stronger, healthier, more vibrant society.

The 2015 Serpentine Pavilion is a remarkable structure. Inspired by its surroundings in Kensington Gardens, yet fabricated from cutting-edge materials, the design that selgascano have created is truly 'betwixt and between' and will inspire visitors to explore the interaction between architecture and nature. We are extraordinarily grateful to the Serpentine Galleries and selgascano; without their effort, dedication and vision this unique installation would not have been possible. We hope that you enjoy visiting the Pavilion as much as we have enjoyed being part of its genesis.

Michael S. Sherwood
Richard J. Gnodde

Co-Chief Executive Officers
Goldman Sachs International

# Directors' Foreword

The Serpentine is delighted to celebrate the fifteenth year of the Galleries' annual Pavilion commission with a design by Spanish architects selgascano. Engaging with selgascano's work – which is characterised by distinctive bold colours, dynamic shapes and a play of light and shadow – is an immersive and sensory experience. As seen in this year's Pavilion, their structures use various synthetic materials and new technologies, which underscore their exploration and experimentation within the field of architecture.

The design of the Serpentine Pavilion 2015 is a dazzling structure made from steel and a multi-coloured fluorine-based polymer (ETFE). This material is both transparent and reflective, and allows visitors to engage with its changing nature – how the light transforms the space from morning to night, and the way light and colour is reflected during the course of a day. The architects' inspiration not only came from the site in Kensington Gardens itself, but from the ways in which people move through London, notably the Underground with its many-layered, chaotic yet structured flow. The Pavilion has multiple entrances and inner walkways, offering a number of ways to stroll through and experience the colourful shell.

José Selgas and Lucía Cano, who formed the practice selgascano in 1998 in Madrid, have completed the majority of their buildings in Spain. The Pavilion resonates with selgascano's earlier projects: the amorphous *Plasencia Auditorium and Congress Centre*; the light-filled harbour-side structure of *El 'B'. Cartagena Auditorium and Congress Centre*; their transparent and colourful home and studio space imbedded in the natural surroundings in Madrid; and the playful, open and multi-functional *Factory Mérida*. The 2015 Pavilion showcases selgascano's deep understanding of the flow of movement in a building, how light changes and is manipulated, the importance of a structure's surroundings, and of how to create a sensorial and memorable experience within architecture.

Each summer the Serpentine invites an internationally renowned architect to create their first built structure in England. The immediacy of the process – a maximum of six months from invitation to completion – provides a unique model for commissioning architecture. The selection of the architects, chosen for consistently expanding the boundaries of architecture practice, is led by the Serpentine's core curatorial thinking, introducing contemporary architects to a wider audience. The brief is to design a 300 square metre Pavilion that is used as a café by day and a forum for learning, debate and entertainment at night. There is no budget for the project: it is realised through sponsorship, help-in-kind support and the sale of the Pavilion. Previous Serpentine Pavilions have been designed by Smiljan Radić (2014), Sou Fujimoto (2013), Herzog & de Meuron and Ai Weiwei (2012), Peter Zumthor (2011), Jean Nouvel (2010), Kazuyo Sejima and Ryue Nishizawa, SANAA (2009), Frank Gehry (2008), Olafur Eliasson and Kjetil Thorsen (2007), Rem Koolhaas and Cecil Balmond, with Arup (2006), Álvaro Siza and Eduardo Souto de Moura with Cecil Balmond, Arup (2005) MVRDV with Arup (2004, unrealised), Oscar Niemeyer (2003), Toyo Ito and Cecil Balmond with Arup (2002), Daniel Libeskind with Arup (2001), and Zaha Hadid, who designed the inaugural Pavilion in 2000.

Each Pavilion also operates as a public space and as a venue for the Serpentine's *Park Nights* programme. Theatre, dance, choreography, film and music all feature in this year's live commissions by artists Fleur Melbourn, Marianna Simnett, Jesse Darling and Christodoulos Panayiotou. The year's series also includes performances by composer Christian Wolff with Apartment House ensemble, choreographer Mette Ingvartsen, and an evening dedicated to the fiftieth anniversary of the legendary International Poetry Incarnation, with poet Michael Horovitz.

First and foremost, the Serpentine would like to offer its heartfelt thanks to José Selgas and Lucía Cano for their commitment and engagement with this project. The playful and innovative design of this year's Pavilion is a testament to their extraordinary vision, creating a unique structure to celebrate the fifteenth year of the commission. The Galleries also extends its thanks to the team at selgascano for all their hard work and dedication on this project, especially Bárbara Bardín and María Levene.

The Lars Windhorst Foundation has very generously, for the second year, supported the summer season across the Serpentine Galleries for which we are immensely thankful.

The Serpentine is enormously grateful to Goldman Sachs, the headline sponsor of the Serpentine Pavilion 2015, who made the wonderful commitment to support the fifteenth anniversary of the commission. The team at Goldman Sachs has been invaluable in realising this collaboration with the Galleries and the Serpentine thanks them.

The Serpentine is truly indebted to its longstanding advisors, the ingenious David Glover, and AECOM: Thomas Webster, Michael Orr, Jack Wilshaw and Katja Leszczynska, whose continued dedication to the Pavilion and their expertise is fundamental to the realisation of the commission. The Serpentine also extends sincere thanks to its collaborator and sponsor Stage One, in particular Ted Featonby and Alan Doyle who work closely with the architects and the Serpentine each year to create the structure.

The commission would not have been possible without support from Weil, Grangewood, Davidson Kempner Capital Management LP, DP9, The Graham Foundation for Advanced Studies in the Fine Arts, Site Engineering Surveys Ltd (SES), The Technical Department Ltd, Total Security Services and WEP, along with the support of the Pavilion Patrons: Gumuchdjian Architects and Thomas Dane. Arts Council England provides an essential contribution towards all of the Galleries' work, for which the Serpentine continues to be grateful. The Serpentine would also like to take the opportunity to thank Richard and Ruthie Rogers for their constant advice, support and enthusiasm over the course of the Pavilion series.

The Serpentine is delighted to present this catalogue to accompany the 2015 Pavilion, which includes a section charting the building and development of this year's design from conception to realisation, together with a text by architecture curator Pedro Gadanho, which considers the vocabulary of selgascano's previous buildings and practice. The publication celebrates the commission's quindecinnial with an essay by architect and writer Sarah Ichioka, which documents the trajectory and history of the series.

Thanks to the Serpentine team Julie Burnell, Head of Projects and Buildings, Jochen Volz, Head of Programmes, Emma Enderby, Exhibitions Curator and Melissa Blanchflower, Assistant Curator who have worked closely with the wider Serpentine Galleries staff to realise this project.

Lastly, the Serpentine Galleries would like to thank the many wonderful architects and their teams, as well as individuals and organisations who have made such an immensely important contribution to the past fifteen years of this commission. Without their dedication this challenging and ambitious series would not have reached this important milestone.

Julia Peyton-Jones
Director, Serpentine Galleries and Co-Director, Exhibitions and Programmes

Hans Ulrich Obrist
Co-Director, Exhibitions and Programmes and Director of International Projects

# selgascano in conversation

**with Julia Peyton-Jones and Hans Ulrich Obrist**

**selgascano**

We don't know if this is a good way to start, but we have a question for you. It's a question that everybody continuously asks us and we don't know what to say: why were we selected for the Serpentine Pavilion?

**Julia Peyton-Jones**

It's a reverse takeover! Well, it's a difficult question because there isn't one answer, but we can try to explain it, and I'll start by detailing the process, which is the same process by which we choose our artists for exhibitions and projects. We have a continual expanding list of people whom we're considering; we research their work and we travel to see it. And because we're not experts in architecture, we also discuss it with our colleagues in the architectural world, asking for their advice and who they're looking at. The initial list of architects we consider is very long, so we refine and refine and refine, and review and review and review, and then we make the decision.

**Hans Ulrich Obrist**

Another important element is our interest in a new generation of architects – those not yet household names in Britain, like Sou Fujimoto in 2013 and then Smiljan Radić last year. One very important inspiration for us was the 2010 Venice Architecture Biennale curated by Kazuyo Sejima, where we spent a lot of time and first encountered your work, Sou's and Smiljan's. We were both very struck by this exhibition: it really offered spaces for experience.

And then there's the organic element, which is difficult to explain. There's always the search to find something that's really relevant, or a practice that redefines how you understand space and how you understand circulation in the space, how you understand the inside-out, how people interact together. This is especially key given the context of the piece of land outside our Gallery. We have to ask ourselves: 'Are these architects suited to doing interesting temporary experiments?', because not every architect invents in this way. The structures have all introduced very different ways of creating a common space. I think that's important.



Installation view: selgascano, 12th International Architecture Exhibition (Venice Biennale 2010)

Installation view: selgascano, 'Between Air', *SPAINLab*, Spanish Pavilion, 13th International Architecture Exhibition (Venice Biennale 2012)

JPJ

I would say that another key element of your practice is your relationship to nature; the fact that it really is imbued in the very heart of your being. Take your installation of suspended plants in the 2012 Venice Architecture Biennale for example, which really explored the relationship between nature and technology. And also the fact that you use materials in a very particular way, as found objects and – whilst respecting materials – not very preciously; they're everyday materials. Then there's the fact that you have a sympathy with working on very democratic spaces for people; they're spaces for everybody. Also your sensitivity to making spaces that are multi-purpose, multi-functional, but unique. If we look at your home (*Silicon House*, Madrid, 2007) that you designed, which is really quite wonderful, and indeed your studio (*Office in the Woods*, Madrid, 2009), there's a feeling of great ease with the assemblage of architectural languages that I find very compelling. For me, what really made me catch my breath was walking into your auditorium at

Cartagena (*El 'B'. Cartagena Auditorium and Congress Centre*, 2011) where the structure is in fact under water. To create a feeling architecturally that's so vivid that you really are destabilised, it is a great architectural *tour de force*.

As you can see, there's no one answer to this complex question, but I hope that we have offered a sense of our reasoning.

**selgascano**

Yes, absolutely, and it's an important question for us because we feel that the Pavilion not only belongs to us, but also to you, to everyone involved in the process – all the collaborators, from the client to the engineers. We've gone in one direction with you, but with somebody else we may have gone in another direction: the design isn't solely dependent on us.

*Office in the Woods* (Madrid, 2009)

**HUO**

Was there a certain moment of creation, of invention? An epiphany? It would be interesting to hear about the genesis of this project.

**selgascano**

We started with something very simple: a kind of transparent tube that had a very subtle colour. It was more of an art object. As the process developed we realised we had been focusing on this idea of an object,



Overleaf: *Silicon House* (Madrid, 2007)

over architecture, and we needed to consider how it would truly function. Our interests therefore grew into playing with more conventional and architectonic materials, like colour, light and shadow, and then with how you enter the Pavilion, how you stroll around it, inside it and in-between it. The structure became about sensations: giving sensations to the people who visit. It wasn't an epiphany that just arrived instantaneously, but more like a continuous process, because even the epiphany is a collaboration. In all of our projects, epiphanies are shared among the teams we work with, or taken from the literature we're reading, or different filmmakers, or different artists.

At Cartagena, something similar happened. To have the auditorium submerged in water was probably an idea that somebody else proposed. So someone else had that epiphany and we put it in the project. So in that sense we're kind of like burglars! And we are very happy with not inventing things but just adding to other processes.

*El 'B'. Cartagena Auditorium and Congress Centre* (Cartagena, 2011)

**JPJ**

It's fascinating that you came to the commission with no baggage about the project, and hence this axis between your fantasy about the Pavilion and the reality. Perhaps this resulted in a different starting point from the one taken by other architects we have worked with. I'm interested in how you resolved the difference between what you hoped for and the reality. How did you resolve that in your minds and in the final design?

**selgascano**

We've always felt that architecture is more about constraints than about personal creative freedom. But constraints – the money, the visitor's needs, the rain, the UV rays – are very important, because they create the architecture. Therefore, there's never a struggle in our minds between the restrictions and our hopes, because our hopes are equally constraints, which all end up defining the structure. So we always try to arrive completely open, completely free, to any project and work with the constraints to shape it. We're therefore always happy with the result.

**HUO**

As we talk about the constraints of architecture, I'm reminded of the text by Ryue Nishizawa in *El Croquis*. It's very beautiful and discusses this amazing quality of 'floating' in your buildings, which is true of the Pavilion here – there's something very light about it. So even if there are always constraints, it doesn't feel as if your buildings are imprisoned by them. It seems that almost the opposite is the case: they're afloat.

**selgascano**

We believe that when you engage in a project that has less freedom and more obstacles, in the end the result can be much more interesting, since you had to work harder. When everything's possible, it's difficult to know what you really need to achieve. As we worked on this project, we went back to the idea that we liked the most, which was the idea of an object that had just landed, that had just touched the ground. In a way, this idea of something that's just touching the ground has always been present in our buildings. Since the landscape here is a park and we really wanted to allow the park to keep its presence, we made the Pavilion as if it was simply touching the landscape for a brief moment, but could fly away at any time.

**JPJ**

This notion of floating also relates to this quality of lightness and glowing, which is an aspect in all your buildings.

**selgascano**

Yes, that's a very good point because lightness also reflects a respect for the site – and not only for the site but for the surroundings. For us, the surroundings of our buildings and their history must always be respected and a sense of lightness allows us to achieve this.

In the case of the Pavilion, when you told us that this year marked its fifteenth anniversary, this history became very important to us, because it was important to the site and to you. Fifteen is a good celebration. So we wanted to consider the whole history of the commission, and this Pavilion is very much an homage to all of the structures that have gone before.

**JPJ**
In what way?

**selgascano**
Well, the Serpentine Pavilion is a theatre, a social space, a café, it's a multi-functional structure. So starting from this idea of a multi-functional space, we looked back at the history of the commission: how each one brought these factors together into a unified structure. Of course, you never want to repeat anything, but we arrived at many points that were similar to previous projects, and understood the many different ways people have experienced the structure each year: through shape, materials, transparency, reflection, light, nature. We decided to keep all these differing ways to experience the space in the design. So this project is quite complex, because we see it as not just one pavilion but as different pavilions with different feelings and different effects brought together, which for us relate to the history of the commission. It's again a stealing of other ideas from the past that we bring together into this complex piece.

**JPJ**
I'd also say that your design for the Serpentine Pavilion is an homage to your previous work. I can point to some of your earlier structures and see elements reappearing in another form. For example, that marvellous ability to walk in between the two skins in the big auditorium in Cartagena is similar to the layered effect and the passageway that wraps around the Pavilion; the colour that's so present in your buildings; that experience of light and also light being reflected. It seems to me that the architectural language that's been played out in other projects is condensed here into one structure.

**selgascano**
Yes, absolutely. The Pavilion is definitely made with the tools that we have in the studio. Of course, another one of those tools that we use often is transparency or reflection that gives you the feeling of lightness. Looking back, that feeling of lightness is very important, because it's probably one of the main elements that belongs to all of the buildings we've designed.

**HUO**

But also the innovative use of materials is important within your practice, particularly this ETFE, a multicoloured fluorine-based polymer. You've used it before, for the auditorium in Cartagena and for the *Plasencia Auditorium and Congress Centre* (Cáceres, 2005–). ETFE is known to age quickly, and I'm curious about this issue of ageing, which isn't often reflected upon in architecture. How are your buildings going to be in twenty, fifty, a hundred years' time? Does it matter to you that your architecture exists for a very long period, or is it something that by its very nature – because of the materials – is more ephemeral?

*Plasencia Auditorium and Congress Centre* (Cáceres, 2005 –)

**selgascano**

Well, this is a very interesting point, and yes, we are happy with this idea of the ephemeral. Take Frei Otto's *Munich Olympics Stadium* of 1972: the whole roof was made of Perspex, completely transparent and it's clearly aged over time. To us, this is very beautiful, because you experience the passing of time in a building. I think this is very important for architecture, and in fact not only architecture, since we also love to experience that wear in every object we use, from our glasses to our chairs. Even the Eames chair, for example, was made of polyester and fibreglass, so you feel that ageing in these chairs. We like to feel that passing of time. For us it's not only beautiful, in that you don't just experience an object, but also how it's changed – its history.

That history is very important to us. So we love using materials that will age; its not an issue.

JPJ

It's a patina.

selgascano

Yes, it's a patina. It's also important to say that the Pavilion relates to the history and the memory of the people in London – especially the light and the movement through the city, with the Underground being very important in this regard. It's a kind of a stream, with different layers that people move between. That inspired us and we tried to bring that idea of London to this Pavilion. For us, this Pavilion is not complete without people inside it, like the Tube; we need the visitors there to create this constant movement through reflections. That's also why the mirrored effect in the material is important for us.

HUO

Was this mirroring on the ETFE an innovative use of the material?

selgascano

Of course, we love to investigate and experiment with materials, and this is why we work with a variety of industries. We try to use different materials that factories produce, to bring them to architecture. But we don't feel that they're new, or something that we're inventing. We are re-using them within an architectural framework. However, the Pavilion is the first time that you'll see the ETFE with a mirror effect, it's never happened before. So that's probably the most innovative thing in the Pavilion: new ideas for materials.

JPJ

At your home and at the studio you designed nature is literally pressing against your windows. Here, it's much more self-contained and ordered. So on the one hand, it seems obvious that you're going to be sympathetic to the location, because there's grass, there are trees, but on the other hand I imagine the very manicured park that we're in could have been a challenge. Am I right?

selgascano

For us, nature always comes first and has always inspired us. We tried to work and collaborate with nature in our house and in our studio. Our house and our studio are the result of working with space in a way that allows nature to be free. Here, with the Pavilion, we found ourselves working in a park that was surrounded by a manicured nature, so we've tried to add to this by creating an enhanced nature. Our main inspiration is to generate and transmit sensations in the space we create. So how can one enjoy nature? How can we feel the light at a given moment, or the sounds, like birdsong? It's playing with these different materials: nature, art, the colours, the sun, the light ... these are the things that inspire us. It's also important how the light will change throughout the day. This is the effect that we were looking for: to experience its transformations during the morning, the afternoon, the night, and even when it rains – it's a way to enjoy nature in an artificial way.

**HUO**

What are your other inspirations, aside from nature – the different sources you pull from?

**selgascano**

Our inspiration is very wide. Music is fundamental; food is very important. We live very simple lives, because we're open to everything. We're happy with every type of food, type of design, type of colour. We don't like one colour, we like all of them. We're not afraid to use any type of colour or any type of idea. So inspiration for our projects comes from everywhere!

**JPJ**

Speaking of colour, it seems fundamental to your practice and a very considered tool, but at times you've contradicted this and its importance to your buildings. It would be interesting to hear you discuss this further.

**selgascano**

Colour is significant for us and we don't deny its weight. However, we understand colour as just another element – we work with it as another material. For example, it's just like talking about the structure. There's a structure in all our buildings, and just like colour, it has to be there. Colour is completely mandatory because we need to paint the steel, you always need to decide the colour. A room can be white, and that's a decision, somebody has to decide that. So it's there, and we're making these decisions continuously, but it's so integrated into the whole project that it's nothing important, really. Colour is just one part of the process. Of course, we make many studies about colour, but again, we equally study how to deal with the structure: 'Can this structure be made in another way?'. Within many factors in the building, we try to see every angle. We try to experiment with every material and with every possible shape of the building, to see if one way is more suited to a particular function than another.

*El 'B'. Cartagena Auditorium and Congress Centre* (Cartagena, 2011)

**JPJ**

It's something that you feel very comfortable with, and this is interesting because architects often don't feel so at ease with colour.

**selgascano**

Because it's very difficult. For us, colour also relates to this quality of lightness that we've already discussed. Most architects are preoccupied with creating spaces by using light and shadow. It's monochromatic. We define and form spaces using different colours. This is what gives lightness to buildings. In our structures, there isn't a strong contrast between light and shadow – there isn't a ray of sunlight in one space and darkness in another. We define and form spaces with distinct colours and distinct materials. This is what makes our buildings lighter and less tense: we use colours instead of shadows.

**HUO**

And the floor of the Pavilion is white…

**selgascano**

Yes, and this is fundamental, because it creates a canvas for the whole Pavilion, reflecting the colours, the shadows, the light. Throughout the design process we always agreed that the roof and the floor had to be the same, and so in the end, the floor is a kind of mirror for the

*El 'B'. Cartagena Auditorium and Congress Centre* (Cartagena, 2011)

roof, because every change, every movement is reflected on the floor, so it moves continuously. The roof is static, but the floor is dynamic.

**JPJ**
It's like stained glass in a church, this idea that through light and colour a different kind of context is created, and you do that very comfortably, very easily.

**selgascano**
Someone once commented that we use a lot of colour but that it's always flat colour. Normally we use colour in a flat way because we're expecting other effects to appear on that colour. In the Pavilion the colour isn't flat at all, it's very mixed and very strong. But the main colour is still the white of the floor, because it's the canvas for all the complexity happening around it. So in the end, white, the colour that embodies all the frequencies, all the colours, happens to be the most important colour for the Pavilion.

# Feast: Urban Vernacular Reinvented

**Pedro Gadanho**

Plexiglas, acrylic, polycarbonate, methacrylate, fibreglass, silicon, polyester, ethylene tetrafluoroethylene. Hydroponic fixtures, ampelopsis, jasminoides, and rubber. This is definitely not your typical recipe for architecture – even in its most contemporary strands. Such ingredients form a mixture of synthetic futurism, ecological passion and hi-tech vs. lo-budget that is, at least, unusual. But this is precisely the flavour that first emerges when you try to get a taste of what Spanish architecture practice selgascano is all about. To this exquisite dish of opposing impulses add a pinch of pop sensibility, and only then will you start to understand the conceptual universe from which the 2015 Serpentine Pavilion magically appears.

I.

José Selgas and Lucía Cano established their office in Madrid in 1998. They matured in a context in which highly qualified, experimental architecture was instigated by a late-blooming, well-rooted modernism – a trend subsequently sustained by a solid architectural education and abundant public commissions. Yet their built work came to full fruition only when, as many said, 'the party was already over'.[1] While in the make, their first sizeable structures reverberated with the real-estate bubble and the socio-economic crisis that hit Southern Europe after 2008. As genuine artists, they acted as seismographs measuring the conditions which surrounded them. While they obeyed a desire to renew the sources and references of architectural culture, they highlighted the contexts and situations in which their buildings were inserted. While they rejected the functional standardisation of an architectural modernism that no longer fulfilled its social promise, they embraced the language of everyday urban culture so as to reconquer the ultimate recipients of architecture: not its clients, but its users. During this period, they finished some crucial masterworks that broke away from previous ambitions of architectural permanence, and sought to adapt to an unstable but inevitable 'new normal'.

1. See Nicolai Ouroussoff, 'It Was Fun Till the Money Ran Out', *The New York Times*, 19 December 2008 (accessed 21 May 2015)



*El 'B'. Cartagena Auditorium and Congress Centre* (Cartagena, 2011)

*El 'B'. Cartagena Auditorium and Congress Centre* (Cartagena, 2011)

## 2.

selgascano spent ten years building their hugely praised *El 'B'. Cartagena Auditorium and Congress Centre*, completed in 2011. They took full advantage of the extended design period to explore unlikely off-the-shelf solutions and refine their brand of innovative, easy-to-assemble detailing. Ultimately, the sophisticated facility was achieved at the unbelievably low price of 185 Euro per square metre. While spatially luxurious, this blazing gem of a building turned out to anticipate the need for austerity, while emphasising the enduring relevance of taking a strong cultural and social stand. The *Factory Mérida* took a little less time to erect, but was similarly sensitive in responding to social and economic downturns with a new architectural vocabulary. As I wrote when this youth centre was concluded in 2011, the unexpectedly festive structure had the ability to cater for a disenfranchised and unemployed population – rather than tourists or other affluent urban users – and thus offered 'a peep into the self-redeeming, political future of architecture'.[2] These concerns would continue to infuse the work of selgascano with a healthy, thought-provoking ambiguity. Even where playfulness or slickness took visible precedence, political readings remained inherent to their work.

2. See Pedro Gadanho, 'Critical Playground', *Domus #948* (Editoriale Domus, Milan, 2011) As I noted at the time, selgascano's project in Mérida 'suggested a debate on what our conceptions of public space should be today – and for whom they should be built'.

3.

Beyond the specific typologies and the social circumstances of the few projects that selgascano have realised throughout a career of over fifteen years, there is a blend of architectural themes that emerge again and again in their work, sometimes in apparently contradictory fashion. selgascano have pursued some of the most emblematic features of modernist architecture, and its play on the perceptual and spatial possibilities of new materials. Even if displaying other concerns, their use of synthetic materials evokes the fascination that drove architects such as Ludwig Mies van der Rohe to experiment with glass and steel. On the other hand, however, their architecture rejects the minimalist abstraction that has become a rule of thumb for modernists. Their use of colour and organic form has been determinedly graphic and unashamedly pop. The retro-futuristic appeal of their works purportedly overcomes the abstract grids and patterns that are more easily associated with a Miesian appropriation of cheap industrial materials. This operation is fundamental. Like the surrealist juxtapositions learnt from Rem Koolhaas, such a *modus operandi* defies what purists would like to assume as the proper grammar of modern architecture.

*Factory Mérida* (Mérida, 2011)

## 4.

In their design investigations, selgascano dismantle and reconstruct the bequest of a quite particular, late architectural modernity. In Spain in the late 1980s, the time of their formative years, the local expression of such a legacy[3] combined with seminal publications on postmodernism by Jean-François Lyotard, Paolo Portoghesi and Fredric Jameson.[4] The mix provided both rich intellectual nourishment and good reasons for a strong critique of modernism. This was the now mostly forgotten moment in which factions of neo-modernist architects with a critical and regional accent fought – and mostly obliterated – their postmodern counterparts. In different contexts, this was also the moment that set the tone for the extremely diversified, stellar definition of the current international status quo in architecture. Coming from a background of philosophers and architects – José belongs to the family of Spanish poet José Selgas, Lucía is the daughter of architect Julio Cano Lasso – it is easy to guess that, from early on, these were architects torn between Mies van der Rohe and Robert Venturi.[5] They were caught between the attraction of a cherished avant-garde tradition, and the repulsion of an architecture gone astray into disciplinary autonomy *and* market commodification.

## 5.

Out of a moment in which the fundamentals of modern architecture were truly questioned there came contemporary practices that, for many, can still seem puzzling and conflicting. At their best, such practices both absorbed the teachings of their modern masters[6] and rejected many of the orthodoxies such masters had professed. Knowledgeable admirers

3. selgascano are often described as continuing themes of historical modernists such as Alejandro de la Sota. As David Cohn points out about the Cartagena auditorium, 'the straightforward massing and simple, ingenious detailing of selgascano's building belongs to a Spanish tradition of low-tech functional design that can be traced back to Alejandro de la Sota's work in the 1950s and '60s, and to the early minimalist work of Abalos and Herreros in the 1990s'. However, 'unlike many of their predecessors, selgascano take realism and solemnity out of low-cost tech and approach it instead as a liberating opportunity for playful invention'. See David Cohn, 'Plane Sailing', *Architectural Review*, April, Northampton, 2012, pp.30–9.

4. See Jean-François Lyotard, *La Condition postmoderne: Rapport sur le savoir* (Minuit, Paris, 1979); Paolo Portoghesi, *Dopo l'Architettura Moderna* (Editori Laterza, Roma, 1980); Fredric Jameson, *Postmodernism, or, The Cultural Logic of Late Capitalism* (Duke University Press, Durham, 1991)

5. Robert Venturi used an investigation into historical architecture to produce one of the earlier critiques of the simplification and standardisation of the Modern Movement in architecture. See Robert Venturi, *Complexity and Contradiction in Architecture* (Museum of Modern Art Press, New York, 1966)

6. As the architecture critic from *El País* wrote, even selgascano's ability to transform poverty of resources in architectural richness is inherited from Spanish modern masters such as Miguel Fisac, Alejandro de la Sota and Alfons Soldevila. See Anatxu Zabalbeascoa, 'El B, una revolución arquitectónica', *El País*, 10 December 2011, Madrid.

of their precedents, disciples with self-governing passions, rebels with a cause, selgascano belong to the first generation of practitioners who gained full critical distance from the International Style – *and* its discontents. Immersed in the globalised culture of technological hype, economic disparity and social unrest, they were eventually forced to come to terms with contradictions that went well beyond the embrace of formal dichotomies once implied by Venturi. Caught in the midst of a fast-evolving and increasingly artificial urban culture, they were the sons and daughters of brilliant thinkers such as Spanish theorist Ignasi de Solà-Morales. Consequently, they became the pursuers of an urban vernacular that no longer relates to past models or pastoral references. If one wants to decipher projects such as their Serpentine Pavilion, one should look through the lens of this viewpoint.

## 6.

As any good dictionary will define, the term 'vernacular' points to a common speech that reflects local, everyday circumstances, rather than standard canons or literary traditions. Jargon and slang are good examples of such popular language. When it comes to architecture, the vernacular may reflect local needs and materials, or the ordinary style of a particular time and place, in contrast to highbrow or monumental architectural expressions. Yet at a time in which the blurring of boundaries between high and low culture have become the norm, these clear definitions become unstable. This may explain why, from the field of film to that of photography or architecture, an apparently contradictory notion of 'vernacular modernism' has gained a certain momentum.[7] Similarly, current notions of 'urban vernacular' would denote a media-infused, pop-culture-driven shift in contemporary architectural expression. This particular form of vernacular has lost all connection to rural or indigenous traditions while simultaneously

7. In film, the term was coined by American critic Miriam Hansen to explain how popular Hollywood cinema functioned as a language that helped people come to terms with ideas of modernity. In photography, the term is associated to photographers such as Walker Evans, when they engage with the language of commercial, everyday life photography. In architecture, some have referred to Aldo van Eyck, Paolo Soleri, Christopher Alexander, or more recently Samuel Mockbee, of Rural Studio, as proponents of 'vernacular architecture' – in a sense that can only be identified with a hybrid notion of 'modern vernacular'. For recent literature on the subject see, for example, Maiken Umbach and Bernd Hüppauf, *Vernacular Modernism* (Stanford University Press, Berkeley, 2005)

moving beyond an academic, mainstream perpetuation of the modern language of architecture. It is at this juncture that one can situate the work of selgascano.

## 7.

As embodied in the work of selgascano, one can trace the emergence of the urban vernacular in contemporary architecture to two main foundations. First, there was the absorption of the industrial vernacular into the very core of architectural modernism. This happened not only in the 1950s in the Miesian sublimation of standardised materials, but also earlier, in the 1920s, when Le Corbusier and others drew inspiration for a new architectural aesthetics from budding urban typologies such as factories and mechanical vessels. By the end of this digestive process, the industrial vernacular had morphed into a proper architectural highbrow, which was to be distanced from mass culture and 'non-pedigreed architecture'.[8] Second, by the 1960s, in the wake of critical revisions of an established modernist lexicon, came the brief love affair of architecture neo-avant-gardes with pop culture – just before postmodernist architects turned their fancy to historicist and neoclassical sources. Shortly after Venturi hailed 'commercial vernacular' and 'learning from Las Vegas',[9] practices such as Archigram, Archizoom or Superstudio used pop imagery and a new urban vernacular to produce critiques of consumer society and prevailing city models. Even if dormant, these trends lingered – and have recently found reason to play out again.

## 8.

Playfulness is a term repeatedly used by critics when addressing the works of selgascano. It is certainly a feature that migrates from the *Factory Mérida* to the Serpentine Pavilion. The use of bright colours and raw organic shapes evoke a festive, childlike imagery, a Miró-esque quality – if not an iconography directly linked to urban festivals. The same Chinese dragon that is discernible in the *Factory Mérida* design

8. See Bernard Rudofsky, *Architecture Without Architects: A Short Introduction to Non-Pedigreed Architecture* (University of New Mexico, Albuquerque, 1964)

9. See Robert Venturi, Steven Izenour & Denise Scott Brown, *Learning from Las Vegas* (MIT Press, Cambridge MA, 1972). In many aspects, the work of Venturi and his colleagues followed on the thesis of Herbert Gans, an American sociologist whose work contributed to undermine distinctions and value judgments opposing highbrow culture and popular culture. This kind of analysis ultimately accompanied the appreciation and legitimation of vernacular expressions produced by mass culture.

is reborn in chrysalid form in the London Pavilion. Such resemblances could suggest the naiveté of a purely vernacular joy, but instead they exemplify an appropriation of recognisable popular imagery so as to seize an urban audience.[10] In Mérida, the adoption of the physical urban jargon that is typical of youth culture – graffiti-covered surfaces, skate ramps, escalating walls, the materials of a disposable plastic culture – help entice a bored, jaded audience. In London, the combination of organic components with the semi-psychedelic translucency of artificial materials induces an enhanced perception of nature, a sort of futuristic celebration of environmental qualities, which is prone to move both children and adults. Beyond populist playfulness, however, this also hints at a deliberate use of pop vernacular to reconnect architecture to its users.

*Educational and Medical Pavilion* project with Massachusetts Institute of Technology (Turkana, Kenya, 2014)

10. As Mario Ballesteros proposed, selgascano 'is pop architecture in the truest sense: architecture for the people. Architecture to be used, lived, enjoyed and occupied'. As Ballesteros also points out, to achieve this they take 'their cues' from the urban setting in a 'neoartisanal' manner. See Mario Ballesteros, 'A new glow in boomtown', in *Domus #954* (Editoriale Domus, Milan, 2012)

Model of unrealised *Twenty Jardin Villas* (Vallecas, 2008)

9.

When it comes to architectural shape, there is a curious antecedent to selgascano's Serpentine Pavilion: an unrealised project for *Twenty Jardin Villas* in Vallecas, 2008. In this design, a cocoon made of metal mesh and colourful vegetation enveloped and determined an idea of dwelling. The concept proposed an interstitial space between houses and their green envelope – a screen guarding home from 'real' nature. Aligning with tendencies *en vogue*, selgascano's research probed briefly into the possibility of using living elements as a building material. In time, however, this desire was firmly substituted by a mounting conviction that architecture was indeed artificial, and that its environmental strategies should rely in the use of man-made, locally sourced, banal materials. Following this logic, instead of a simple emulation of the natural world, their Serpentine Pavilion offers a twisted, experiential relationship with the surrounding landscape. It reiterates architecture's essential role as an environmental filter, while it feasts on the effusive possibilities of future synthetic materials. It says that, ultimately, these materials will be not only cheaper, but also more ecological in their performance.[11] It says that these materials – rather than stone, wood or glass – are the right constituents for a new, resourceful vernacular.

11. As described by José Selgas, materials such as methacrylate are 'more sustainable than glass, 100% recyclable as opposed to 50% in the case of glass, more economical, and much more insulating'. See Zabalbeascoa, idem.

selgascano employ playfulness to trigger political and ecological assertions. Their work for the Serpentine has been pleasantly and deceitfully described as a fun-filled 'visitor experience'. Yet readings of this colourful architecture should dig beyond its translucent surfaces. Embracing popular appeal,[12] selgascano have raised enough questions – and addressed enough concerns – to reassure us that an innocent pavilion may distill an alternative political vision. In a recent interview, they quoted Zygmunt Bauman to advance an apparently nihilistic position: 'Nothing is necessary.'[13] They did not mean to surrender to the pervasive assumption that artists and architects do not affect change. On the contrary, they were underlining the fact that creative endeavours must rely on 'doing less'. Architecture should increasingly be about consuming fewer natural resources, and leaving less of an ecological imprint. In this sense, selgascano integrate a wave of architects who foster an out-of-the-box take on sustainable design.[14] Through this, architecture can return to a vernacular attitude of radical, if playful, adaptation to context.[15] Some started to call this Vernacular 2.0. I prefer to think of it as urban vernacular reinvented.[16] This is what will eventually produce relevant change – and selgascano affirm it with a Pavilion that is simply … cool.

12. As they point out in their own profile, 'selgascano avoid the use of games and mechanisms that lead to disciplinary issues, and strive to seek beauty that is comprehensible to any human being', in José Selgas & Lucía Cano, *El Croquis #171* (Croquis Editorial, Madrid, 2014)

13. See Edwin Heathcote, 'selgascano, the architects behind the next Serpentine Pavilion', *Financial Times*, 26 December 2014, London.

14. See the winning proposals for the *Young Architects Program*, at MoMA PS1, New York, where the range of experimental concepts for temporary outdoor installations included pollution-eating nanoparticles, upcycling from industrial waste, zero-emission bio-bricks and, most recently, a festive take on the scarcity and purification of water by Madrid-based Andrés Jaque Arquitectos / Office for Political Innovation.

15. This attitude should not refrain to urban contexts in the developed world. On the contrary, it bears even more sense in contexts in which resources are extremely scarce. José Selgas has already understood this when bringing MIT students to develop their skills in extracting maximum effects out of specific materials and vernacular techniques in the context of a project in Kenya. See Tomà Berlanda, in 'Shade of Meaning: Clinic in Turkana, Kenya', *The Architectural Review*, February, London, 2015.

16. As I see it, this notion of urban vernacular relates to contemporary practices that source references and materials from their immediate urban context. For an analysis of this tendency, see Pedro Gadanho, 'Open-Source Architecture', *A10 #07*, January – February, Amsterdam, 2006.

SERPENTINE GALLERY

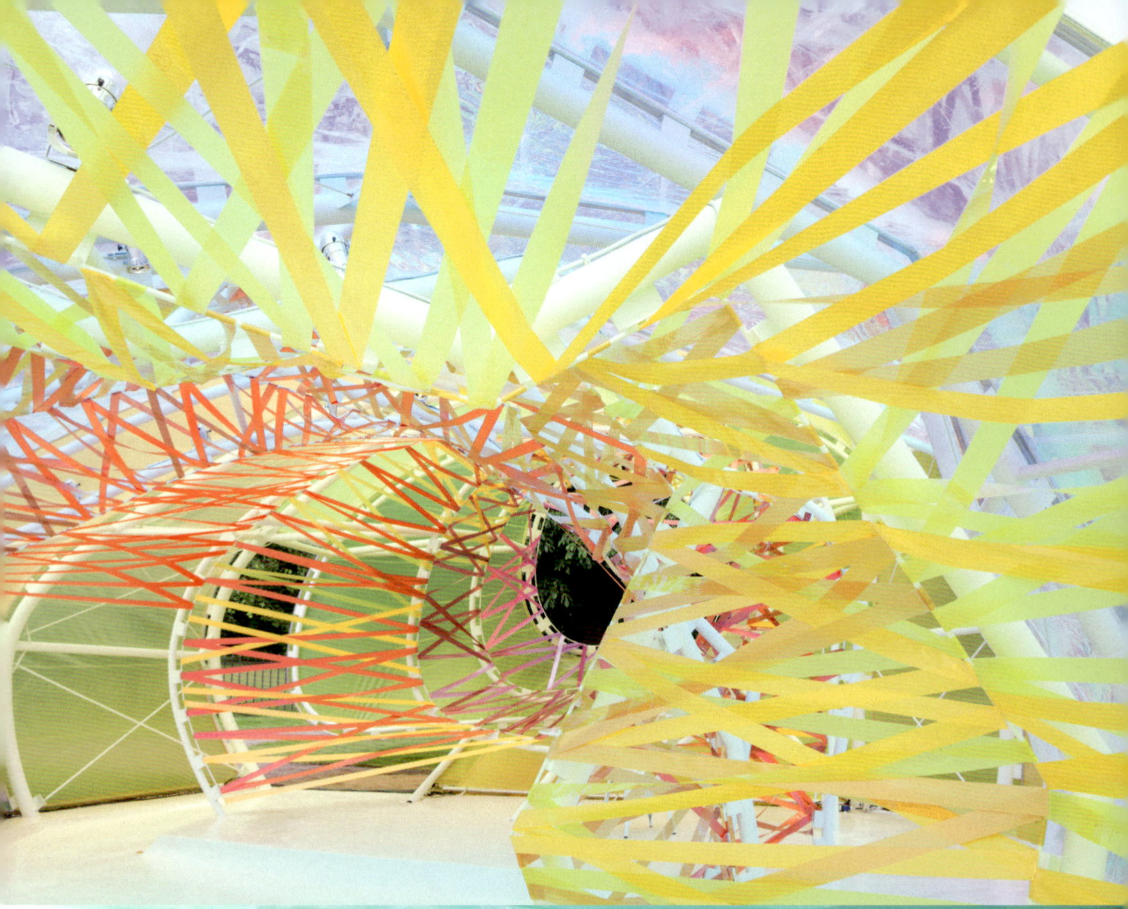

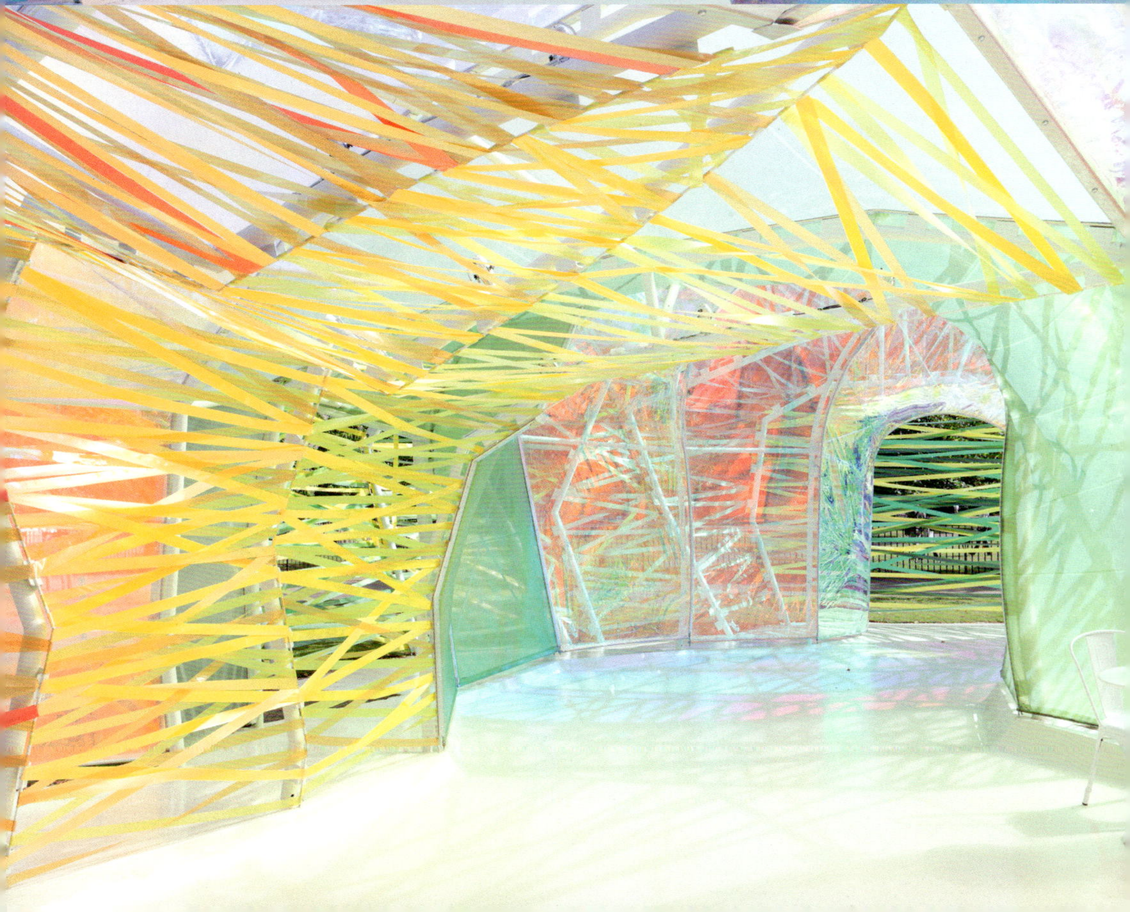

# Patronage, Persuasion and the Public:

# Fifteen Years of the Serpentine Pavilion

Sarah Ichioka

The original Serpentine Pavilion issued from a happy confluence of circumstances and actors. On the occasion of the Serpentine Gallery's thirtieth anniversary in 2000, Director Julia Peyton-Jones asked the architect Zaha Hadid to design a temporary structure to host a gala dinner, one that would 'reinvent the accepted idea of a tent or marquee' whilst remaining within the budget of a hired-in structure. Hadid's design was intended to stand for only one night, but Chris Smith, the Secretary of State for Culture, Media and Sport, attending the gala dinner, liked it so much that he pulled strings to allow it to remain in place for public enjoyment, catered for by a hastily sourced café operator, for the remainder of the summer.[1]

The spontaneous success of Hadid's temporary structure inspired a series of annual pavilions commissioned from design teams, including architects, engineers, artists and a landscape architect, drawn from over a dozen nationalities, leading up to the most recent, Spanish firm selgascano, in 2015. The series, perhaps most noticeably in its early iterations, has been driven by a strong campaigning mission: to introduce to a London public the work of acknowledged international masters of contemporary architecture who had not yet built in England.[2] In the course of fifteen summers, the Serpentine Pavilion has hosted an estimated four million visitors and over 200 public events, becoming a fixture of London's cultural calendar and arguably the best-known product of its parent institution.

1. The Serpentine had commissioned temporary event structures from designers in 1998 and 1999, but Hadid's was the first to enjoy this extended public life. Philip Jodidio, '2000 Zaha Hadid', *Serpentine Gallery Pavilions* (Taschen, Cologne, 2011) I.06.

2. The brief has been adjusted over the years to accommodate new circumstances and curatorial prerogatives, but its core principles endure.



Aerial view of Serpentine Pavilion 2015, designed by selgascano

Above and opposite: Kensington Gardens Old Tea House, built 1934

From a historical perspective, Kensington Gardens is a natural place for such a project to originate and flourish. The Gardens, adjoining Hyde Park and close to some of London's most privileged neighbourhoods, have grown through a history of royal patronage, including landscape interventions such as the Serpentine lake, commissioned by Queen Caroline in the 1730s, as well as temporary structures, the most well-known of which was Joseph Paxton's Crystal Palace at the Great Exhibition of 1851, a swiftly designed feat of architectural innovation, through which 'the Park became the showcase for the Industrial Revolution and cabinet of wonders for the English Empire'.[3] This legacy endures in the world-class educational and cultural institutions along Exhibition Road, to the Serpentine's south. Following a parallel history as a place for dissent and political speech, the Royal Parks have in more recent years become a site for popular events from concerts to sport, and for the erection of sculptural memorials. The Serpentine Gallery itself was originally a site of leisure: a tea pavilion designed in 1934 by J. Grey West, chief architect for HM Office of Works. The Grade II listed building was repurposed at the behest of the Arts Council of England in 1970 for the exhibition of contemporary art.[4] Themes from this history – of privilege and public participation, city and landscape, heritage and innovation, leisure and politics – recur in the Serpentine's current public programmes and private patronage.

3. Leo Hollis, 'A Place Necessary for Everyone', *Serpentine Galleries website* (accessed 15 May 2015)

4. Ibid.

OUT
IN

In its early years, the Serpentine Pavilion initiative benefitted from London's political and economic environment, which at the turn of the millennium was remarkably fecund for the creation of bold cultural projects. New Labour, having won landslide elections in 1997 and 2001, prioritised funding for the arts as a booster for Britain's international profile. Frieze Art Fair (established in 2003) asserted London's position as a commercial hub for contemporary art. Three now iconic buildings were just taking their place on London's skyline: Tate Modern (2000), the London Eye (2000) and 30 St Mary Axe – 'the Gherkin' (2003). The first directly elected Mayor of London, Ken Livingstone, took office in 2000, followed by a burst of investment in local infrastructure and public spaces, of which the pedestrianisation of the National Gallery side of Trafalgar Square was perhaps the most visible (2003). Within popular media, programmes like *Grand Designs* (first broadcast in 1999) familiarised viewers with the basics of contemporary architecture.

Installation view: Tadashi Kawamata, *Inside Out* (Serpentine Gallery, 1997)

Peyton-Jones has described the Pavilion as a 'natural evolution from earlier projects'.[5] The 1998 renovation of the Gallery by museum specialists architects John Miller and Partners appears to have spurred the subsequent Pavilion project in both positive and negative ways. During the renovations, the Serpentine curated a well-received

5. Philip Jodidio, 'Interview with Julia Peyton-Jones and Hans Ulrich Obrist', *Serpentine Gallery Pavilions*, (Taschen, Cologne, 2011) p.8.

programme of commissions called *Inside Out*, in which artists including Richard Deacon, Tadashi Kawamata and Anya Gallaccio responded directly to the Gallery building and its setting. However, the experience of the renovation itself, a 'construction-management' arrangement, moved Peyton-Jones to comment publicly that the process 'kept us at arm's length from the architects. It was the antithesis of how we work as a Gallery with artists, which is collaboratively [...] The construction management process patently did not deliver what it promised. Furthermore, it underscored our powerlessness as the client.'[6] In contrast to this experience, Peyton-Jones positioned the Serpentine Pavilion as an alternative, 'curatorial' approach to commissioning architecture: 'What we do at the Serpentine is to display objects, and we see the pavilion as a super-sized object. We bring the model of working with artists, of commissioning, collaborating, enabling, encouraging, translating, facilitating, shaping and guiding to the process of working with architects. We set out to achieve their vision.'[7]

The 2000 Hadid prototype and the preferred 'curatorial' approach commissioning established the characteristics of the brief for subsequent pavilions. These include *Simplicity*: 'The lack of a complex brief is one of the key characteristics of the project. The pavilion is in essence a container that need not contain. The structure itself has no services to speak of'.[8] They also include *Speed*: approximately six months are allowed between the architect's invitation and the pavilion's opening, with the final work open to the public for three to four months; *Authorship*: the commission mandates the direct involvement of the principal designer or designers instead of delegation to juniors; yet also, *Collaboration*: a number of the pavilions have been designed by named teams – two architects, architect and engineer, artist and architect – many of whom have expressed a disregard for disciplinary boundaries. Collaboration is also a necessary reality because many of the professional services for each pavilion are provided as in-kind support; the project 'relies upon the generosity of all involved and only works because everyone has to take a leap of faith'.[9] Finally, *Transferability* is a quiet yet essential element of the commissioning formula, each 'super-sized object' being sold and reproduced or relocated to recoup up to 40% of its production costs, particularly important to the Serpentine as the commission receives no public funding.[10]

6. Julia Peyton-Jones, 'Fast Forward Architecture', *Serpentine Gallery Pavilion 2005; Designed by Alvaro Siza, Eduardo Souto De Moura with Cecil Balmond – Arup*, ed. Melissa Larner (Serpentine Gallery and Trolley, London, 2005) p.30.

7. Ibid., p.26.

8. Ibid., p.40.

9. Ibid., p.30.

10. The 2010 Pavilion by Jean Nouvel, supported by a 'Sustain' grant from the Arts Council of England, was the exception.

Serpentine Pavilion 2000, designed by Zaha Hadid

The Serpentine Pavilion commission is founded on Peyton-Jones's premise that the best way to convince the public of the merits of contemporary architecture is to present it in a format that is immersive and experiential, rather than a traditional architectural exhibition of drawings and models, and also enjoyable: an environment in which 'everyone' feels comfortable entering and lingering – hence the absence of doors (and often, of walls) amongst the pavilions, the consistent presence of a café vendor within, and the relative absence of docents and didactic texts. Each pavilion must address at least three distinct audiences: it must be accessible enough to attract large public audiences including casual passersby, meeting the expectations of its governmental and charitable funders; it must be flexible enough to be configured to host public programmes ranging from lectures to musical performances, meeting the needs of the culturally engaged; and it must be sufficiently glamorous to host what *Vogue* has called 'one of the great parties of the London season',[11] important for the Gallery's social profile and associated financial support.

Another ambition, perhaps becoming more pronounced as the Serpentine's need to justify the Pavilion series has receded with each successful iteration, is that the commission might stimulate new approaches to architectural practice, both in terms of the individual architect's career trajectory and through the impact of each pavilion on the discourse of his or her professional peers. Peyton-Jones asserts,

11. Virginia Bates, 'Serpentine Time', *Vogue UK*, 15 July 2009 (accessed 15 May 2015)

'The pavilion's temporality and the extremely fast programme can provoke architects into experimentation. As well as being encapsulations of their creators' oeuvres, the pavilions can also act as a significant spur to the expansion of their ideas, while conventional buildings can often stifle ambition.'[12] This ambition – what one might call the incubator motive – is historically grounded in the impact of temporary exhibition structures on the development of modern architecture, compellingly chronicled by Beatriz Colomina.[13] Just two examples of many such temporary projects with lasting cultural impact are Mies van der Rohe's German Pavilion for the 1929 Barcelona International Exhibition, and Alison and Peter Smithson's *The House of the Future* for the 1956 Daily Mail Ideal Home Exhibition, London. The incubator motive evolved with the 2006 arrival of Hans Ulrich Obrist as Serpentine Gallery Co-Director, who brought to the Pavilion project his interest in the cross-pollination of ideas between disciplines and between arts institutions and the wider world.

Serpentine Pavilion 2002, designed by Toyo Ito

Following the lead of the Hadid prototype, commissions from Daniel Libeskind (2001) and Toyo Ito (2002) shared an interest in visually striking and novel geometries enabled by the computer-aided design tools that had become increasingly influential in architecture from the 1980s

12. Peyton-Jones, *op. cit.*, pp.34–5

13. Beatriz Colomina, 'Pavilions of the Future', *Frank Gehry: Serpentine Gallery Pavilion 2008*, ed. Kathryn Rattee (Koenig and the Serpentine Gallery, London 2008) p.74.

onwards. They also share evident delight in finding engineering solutions to realise these; all three were produced in collaboration with the structural engineer Cecil Balmond and his team at Arup.

Oscar Niemeyer (2003) and the collaborative team of Alvaro Siza and Eduardo Souto de Mouro (2005) were architects of well-established reputation whose Pavilion designs were influenced by human and animal forms respectively. On the other end of the age spectrum came MVRDV (2004), playing the role of the radical young provocateurs since in the end their design, which sought to cover the existing Serpentine Gallery with an inhabitable topography, was not built due to issues with the planning permission and the high cost.

'Interview Marathon' taking place inside the Serpentine Pavilion 2006, designed by Rem Koolhaas and Cecil Balmond, with Arup

A shift occurred in 2006, when the Pavilion by Rem Koolhaas and Cecil Balmond coincided with the addition of Obrist to the commissioning team. This Pavilion, whose inflatable roof emphasised its ephemerality, privileged the events programming, and introduced the format of the thematic 'Marathon', which joined the continuing *Park Nights* programme of public events to become a key feature of the annual commission. Artist Olafur Eliasson and architect Kjetil Thorsen (2007) also emphasised the experience of the Pavilion's internal environment and expanded the Marathon format with a link to events in Berlin, underscoring the fluidity of both disciplinary and geographic boundaries in contemporary creative practice. Frank Gehry's Pavilion (2008) might be grouped with earlier Serpentine commissions, given the architect's reputation for dramatic forms enabled by advanced digital technologies. However, Gehry also embraced the expanded brief, designing his Pavilion to host performances, particularly the opening performance by composer Thomas Adès.

Serpentine Pavilion 2009, designed by Kazuyo Sejima and Ryue Nishizawa of SANAA

In the wake of the 2008 Global Financial Crisis, one might have found easy metaphors for societal excess in the forms of the preceding years' pavilions, as indeed one could with many permanent buildings constructed or planned in that period: 'inflated', 'spiralling', 'over-structured'. In the downturn, London saw fewer cranes on its skyline as the construction industry stalled, and cultural institutions struggled to justify their existence in the face of vanishing funds. Those straitened circumstances offered the opportunity for another shift. The 2009 commission, by SANAA, refocused their Pavilion outwards, on its natural setting, its mirrored surface gently amplifying and integrating with the park landscape. The following designs by Jean Nouvel (2010) and by Peter Zumthor (2011) also responded to the natural setting of Kensington Gardens, albeit in different extremes, the former an extroverted burst of crimson, meant to highlight the greenness of its surroundings, and organised play; the latter soberly cloistered for the contemplation of a flowering garden designed by Piet Oudolf.

Conference call between (left) architects Herzog & de Meuron and (right) artist Ai Weiwei, 2012

In 2010, at the Serpentine Pavilion's ten-year mark, one could reflect upon how much progress had been made in the Gallery's campaign to persuade Londoners to embrace contemporary architecture by internationally renowned firms. Prince Charles's controversial intervention to halt contemporary designs at Chelsea Barracks aside, Rem Koolhaas's firm had been commissioned to design the headquarters for Rothschild Bank; Zaha Hadid's London Aquatics Centre, under construction, was tipped to be the star of the Olympic Park; also within the Park, Cecil Balmond was engineering 'the UK's tallest sculpture' with sculptor Anish Kapoor, a pet project of the Mayor, and – perhaps most tellingly – in the same year that Jean Nouvel designed the Serpentine Pavilion, his atelier opened a 560,000 square foot shopping mall and office complex for a commercial property developer, directly facing St Paul's Cathedral.

As to the 'curatorial' approach to architecture, a decade on, Peyton-Jones's argument for the pedagogical and persuasive advantages of immersive temporary commissions over traditional architectural exhibitions appeared to have positively influenced her peers. Amongst many possible examples in England alone, the V&A's *1:1 Architects Build Small Spaces* exhibition (2010), the London Design Festival (founded in 2003, with their 'Landmark Projects' commissions series active since 2007), the Architectural Association's experimental student-designed pavilions at Bedford Square (since 2004) and the Living Architecture initiative (founded 2010), which commissions elite design teams to design accessibly priced holiday homes, all owe a happy debt to the Serpentine. The Pavilion series would continue its evolution in the midst of a global proliferation of architecture and design biennials, triennials and festivals, alongside the venerable tradition of international expos, which use temporary architecture to broadcast competing national and commercial identities and goods.

The Serpentine Gallery, like its London peers, gave special care to its 2012 programing, anticipating the heavier media attention accompanying the Summer Olympic and Paralympic Games, whilst also seeking to complement rather than compete with the spectacles on show in the Olympic Park. The Serpentine's choice of architects Herzog & de Meuron and artist Ai Weiwei, who had collaborated on the National Stadium for the 2008 Beijing Olympics and were already relatively well known to London audiences, stretched the Gallery's own commissioning rules and was arguably a conservative choice. However, the team's familiarity with London may have freed them to devote more attention to the specificities of the site. Their design, based upon the physical foundations of the eleven preceding pavilions, was the first directly to address the history of the commission, seeking these spatial inheritances to shape its own form. The archaeological approach provided a ritual clearing. Although Herzog & de Meuron are of the 'starchitect' class, they adopted a conceptual, visually subdued approach that resonates with the work of an emerging generation of practitioners.

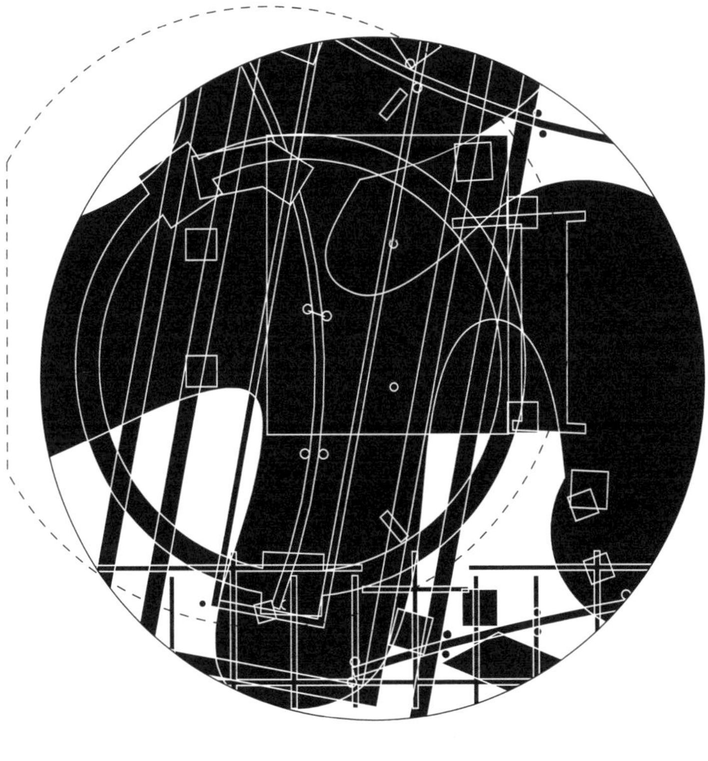

Foundation plan of Serpentine Pavilion 2012, designed by Herzog & de Meuron and Ai Weiwei

According to Obrist, the following two commissioned architects, Sou Fujimoto (2013) and Smiljan Radić (2014), are 'part of a generation that's no longer producing "iconic" architecture' but rather are 'more interested in creating a climatic situation, an atmospheric space',[14] focusing more – the argument goes – on how their buildings 'feel' than how they look. The 2015 Pavilion architects selgascano might also be counted amongst this cohort. In talking about their work, Radić, Fujimoto and selgascano all seem at pains to avoid 'form-making' and 'authorship', although they often generate visually arresting and photogenic forms, a significant if unsought factor in the Instagram era. They approach constraints as essential elements of the design process.

Serpentine Pavilion 2014, designed by Smiljan Radić

It's hard to think of an architect who wouldn't be thrilled to receive a phone call from Peyton-Jones and Obrist. The care that the Serpentine lavishes upon their commissioned architects is certainly to be coveted. And for all its sense of 'and now for something thrillingly new' each summer, an ethic of loyalty and continuity is evident within the Serpentine Pavilion's programme. This can be discerned in the form

14. Hans Ulrich Obrist, 'In Conversation – Smiljan Radić with Julia Peyton-Jones and Hans Ulrich Obrist', *Smiljan Radić: Serpentine Gallery Pavilion 2014*, ed. Emma Enderby and Jochen Volz (Koenig and the Serpentine Galleries, London, 2014) p.39.



Serpentine Pavilion 2013, designed by Sou Fujimoto

of progressive commissions for Zaha Hadid, whose permanent extension to the Serpentine's new Sackler Gallery (2013) shows a clear lineage from the original 2000 commission, via a large-scale sculpture that Hadid designed to host the 2007 Summer Party when the main Pavilion was delayed. In a more subtle line, one can trace ties of mentorship and advocacy between, for example, Toyo Ito, SANAA and Fujimoto, or the fact that the work of Radić, Fujimoto and selgascano featured in the 2010 Venice Biennale curated by SANAA partner Kazuyo Sejima.

In its persuasion-through-immersion campaign, much of the Serpentine Pavilion's cumulative strength has derived from these underlying connections and the reiteration of a simple brief. At the same time, and as might be expected, some of the most significant developments in the Pavilion series have been influenced by external factors. Now, as it advances towards its twentieth year, with both public audiences and private sponsors enthusiastically converted to the cause, the commissioners of the Serpentine Pavilion might enjoy the opportunity to review some of the project's core principles.

The simplicity of the Serpentine's brief has rightly been viewed as a liberating aspect by the architects involved. However, when considering the most recent cohort's interest in the role of constraint in the design process, one wonders whether the unfettered freedom of the brief, consistent with the Serpentine Galleries' enabling, curatorial approach to commissioning, might one day prompt more focused experimentation in answering some of our era's greatest challenges to architects and their clients: how might public spaces address extreme and growing inequalities of resources, mobility and visibility? How do intimacy and identity relate to built form in a digitally networked and surveilled world? What are the true socio-ecological implications of the materials and techniques with which we construct our buildings, and understanding these, how might we build differently? How might we light/heat/cool/irrigate/clean our buildings in a manner that is restorative rather than extractive?[15] selgascano's stated interests in architecturally unconventional materials and in maximising space for nature in their buildings will be interesting to examine in this context.

selgascano also cite the work and words of filmmakers and poets as significant influences on their practice of architecture. How might future Serpentine Pavilion commissions stretch beyond the architecture-art-structural engineering continuum to facilitate collaborations between

15. For comparison, MoMA PS1's Young Architects Program, which has commissioned a temporary summer structure since 2000, requires the provision of water. The 2015 commission by architect Andrés Jacque prototypes a new water purification system.

designers and biologists, coders, anthropologists, activists, or the materials and engineering students of the Royal College of Art and Imperial College just down the road, perhaps even the café operators whose essential job it is to entice passersby into the Pavilion? By setting an expanded agenda for the range of architectural topics to be explored by the Pavilion, the Serpentine's curators would be building upon the commission's solid history of showcasing interdisciplinary collaboration and its public programmes' strong history of knowledge-sharing amongst leading thinkers from the fields of science, literature etc.

By choosing a 'curatorial' commissioning approach, and avoiding public competition, the Serpentine avoids the pain, but also the potential for greater long-term systemic impact that engagement with the disparaged British 'procurement process' might produce. Whilst reform of this nature is neither glamorous nor of obvious popular appeal, the Serpentine's leadership may be uniquely positioned to apply its curatorial sensitivities to shape a more collaborative, respectful, quality enhancing competitive process, distilling and sharing wisdom from their many years of direct commissioning.[16] A review of the portfolio of relatively young practice selgascano, much of whose work developed through European design competitions, reminds the viewer of the powerful incubator role competition can play.

What is lost in mystique may be repaid in insight. In a field increasingly full of attention-seeking temporary structures, a pioneering commissioning programme that invested sufficient time for revolutionary research and development, strove to share accrued knowledge, and directly addressed the demands of changing circumstances might distinguish itself anew.

Thanks to Erin Manns, Abraham Thomas
and Eleanor Johnson.

16. The Architectural Record / Van Alen Institute's 2015 survey of architects' attitudes to competition culture brims with provocative insights and recommendations to clients.



Overleaf: Serpentine Pavilions 2000–14

Zaha Hadid, 2000

Daniel Libeskind, with Arup, 2001

Toyo Ito and Cecil Balmond, with Arup, 2002

Oscar Niemeyer, 2003

Concept for Serpentine Pavilion (unrealised)
Designed by MVRDV with Arup, 2004

Álvaro Siza, and Eduardo Souto de Moura
with Cecil Balmond – Arup, 2005

Rem Koolhaas and Cecil Balmond, with Arup, 2006

Olafur Eliasson & Kjetil Thorsen, 2007

*Lilas*: an installation by Zaha Hadid Architects, Zaha Hadid and Patrik Schumacher, 2007

Frank Gehry, 2008

Kazuyo Sejima and Ryue Nishizawa of SANAA, 2009

Jean Nouvel, 2010

Peter Zumthor, garden design by Piet Oudolf, 2011

Herzog & de Meuron and Ai Weiwei, 2012

Sou Fujimoto, 2013

Smiljan Radić, 2014

José Selgas and Lucía Cano established **selgascano** in Madrid, Spain, in 1998. Both were born in Madrid in 1965 and studied architecture at Escuela Técnica Superior de Arquitectura de Madrid. After graduating in 1992, Selgas worked with Francesco Venecia in Naples, winning the Rome Prize from Academia Española de Bellas Artes de Roma in 1997–8. Cano worked with renowned Spanish architect Julio Cano Lasso and was a member of the studio until 2001.

selgascano's work is characterised by a use of synthetic materials and new technologies. Taking inspiration from Luis Barragán and Richard Rogers, selgascano use distinctive colours and references to nature throughout their designs. selgascano also believe that architecture should be built with a consideration to existing surroundings, which has informed their design course on nature and climatology at Massachusetts Institute of Technology and their work on the *Educational and Medical Pavilion* (Turkana, Kenya, 2014).

selgascano studio has completed the majority of its buildings in Spain through a diverse range of commissions, including *Silicon House* (Madrid, 2007); *Office in the Woods* (Madrid, 2009); *El 'B'. Cartagena Auditorium and Congress Centre* (Cartagena, 2011); and *Factory Mérida* (Mérida, 2011). In 2014 they completed the refurbishment of *Second Home*, London. Current projects include *Plasencia Auditorium and Congress Centre* (Caceres, Spain); *'Pip' House* (Laurel Canyon, Los Angeles); the renovation of *Texas Square* (Oranjestad, Aruba); and *'La Canaria' House* (Mount Washington, Los Angeles). selgascano's work has been exhibited at the Museum of Modern Art and the Solomon R. Guggenheim Museum, New York; GA Gallery and the Museum of Contemporary Art, Tokyo; Design Museum, London; Akademie der Künste, Berlin; Tin Sheds Gallery, Sydney; and Massachusetts Institute of Technology, Boston. The architects were chosen for the Venice Architecture Biennale in 2010, curated by Japanese architect Kazuyo Sejima of SANAA, architects of the Serpentine's 2009 Pavilion, and again for the Biennale's Spanish Pavilion 2012, as part of *SpainLab*, an exhibition that brought together the work of seven Spanish architects. In 2013 they won the Kunstpreis (Art prize) awarded by the Akademie der Künste, Berlin, and were pronounced 'Architects of the Year' by the German Design Council.

**Pedro Gadanho** is the Curator of Contemporary Architecture in the Department of Architecture and Design at the Museum of Modern Art, New York. Since he joined MoMA in 2012, he has been responsible for the *Young Architects Program*, and curated the exhibitions *9+1 Ways of Being Political* (2012–3), *Cut 'n' Paste* (2013–4), *Conceptions of Space* (2014), and *Uneven Growth* (2014–5). Gadanho holds an MA in Art and Architecture and a PhD in Architecture and Mass Media. He is the author of *Interiores 01–010* (2010) and of *Arquitectura em Público* (2011), a recipient of the FAD Prize for Thought and Criticism in 2012. He was the editor of *BEYOND* bookazine, writes the Shrapnel Contemporary blog, and contributes regularly to international publications. He curated *Metaflux* at the 2004 Venice Architecture Biennale and exhibitions such as *Post.Rotterdam* (2001), *Space Invaders* (2001), and *Pancho Guedes – An Alternative Modernist* (2008). He was also a chief curator of ExperimentaDesign, Lisbon between 2001 and 2003. Amongst exhibition layouts, galleries and refurbishments, his designs, situated in Portugal, include *Orange House* (Carreco, 2005); *Family Home* (Oporto, 2005); *Ellipse Foundation* (Lisbon, 2006); and *GMG House* (Torres Vedras, 2010).

**Sarah Ichioka** holds a BA in History from Yale University and an M.Sc. in City Design and Social Science from the London School of Economics. Ichioka has been honoured as a Fellow of the Royal Institute of British Architects, a British Council Cultural Leadership International Fellow, and in 2013 was named one of the Public Interest Design 100. Previous roles include: Director of The Architecture Foundation, London; Co-Director of the London Festival of Architecture; Consultant Curator, Tate Modern, London; Urban Consultant, Witherford Watson Mann Architects, London; Founding Research Associate, The Urban Age Project, London; Content Coordinator and Catalogue Co-Editor, Venice Architecture Biennale; and Community Development Fellow at New York City's Department of Housing. Ichioka has served on numerous boards and juries for projects including the European Prize for Urban Public Space; the selection committee for the British Pavilion at the Venice Biennale; the curatorial committee of the Design Museum, London; the Young Architect of the Year Award, London; and the Rolex Mentor and Protégé Arts Initiative. Her publications include chapters in *The Endless City* (2008); *Mies van der Rohe / European Union Prize for Contemporary Architecture 25th Anniversary* (2013); and *Constructing Worlds: Photography and Architecture in the Modern Age* (2014). Ichioka is currently based in Southeast Asia.

## Credits

p.8
Installation view: selgascano, *People meet in architecture*, 12th International Architecture Exhibition (Venice Biennale 2010)
Photograph © Roland Halbe

p.10
Installation view: selgascano, 'Between Air', *SPAINLab*, Spanish Pavilion, 13th International Architecture Exhibition (Venice Biennale 2012)
Photograph © Nicolás Saieh

p.11
*Office in the Woods* (Madrid, 2009)
Photograph © Iwan Baan

pp.12–3
*Silicon House* (Madrid, 2007)
Photograph © Richard Powers

pp.14; 20–2; 24
*El 'B'. Cartagena Auditorium and Congress Centre* (Cartagena, 2011)
Photographs © Iwan Baan

p.17
*Plasencia Auditorium and Congress Centre* (Cáceres, 2005 – )
Photograph © Hisao Suzuki

p.25; 29
*Factory Mérida* (Mérida, 2011)
Photographs © Iwan Baan

p.30
*Educational and Medical Pavilion* project with Massachusetts Institute of Technology (Turkana, Kenya, 2014)
Photograph © Iwan Baan

p.31
Model of unrealised *Twenty Jardin Villas* (Vallecas, 2008)
© selgascano

pp.33–64
Serpentine Pavilion 2015, designed by selgascano
Photographs © 2015 Iwan Baan

p.68
Installation view: Tadashi Kawamata, *Inside Out* (Serpentine Gallery, 1997)
Photograph © 1997 Tadashi Kawamata

p.70
Serpentine Pavilion 2000, designed by Zaha Hadid
Photograph © Hélène Binet

p.71
Serpentine Pavilion 2002, designed by Toyo Ito
Photograph © Sylvain Deleu

p.72
Interior of the Serpentine Pavilion 2006, designed by Rem Koolhaas and Cecil Balmond, with Arup
Photograph © John Offenbach

p.73
Serpentine Pavilion 2009, designed by Kazuyo Sejima and Ryue Nishizawa of SANAA
Photograph © 2009 Iwan Baan

p.74
Conference call between Herzog & de Meuron and Ai Weiwei
Photograph © 2012 Herzog & de Meuron and Ai Weiwei

p.75
Foundation plan of Serpentine Pavilion 2012
© 2012 Herzog & de Meuron and Ai Weiwei

p.76
Serpentine Pavilion 2013, designed by Sou Fujimoto
Photograph © Jim Stephenson

p.77
Serpentine Pavilion 2014, designed by Smiljan Radić
Photograph © 2014 Iwan Baan

pp.80–1
Serpentine Pavilions 2000–14

Serpentine Pavilion 2000,
designed by Zaha Hadid
Photograph © Hélène Binet

Serpentine Pavilion 2001
*Eighteen Turns,* designed by
Daniel Libeskind, with Arup
Photograph © Hélène Binet

Serpentine Pavilion 2002,
designed by Toyo Ito and
Cecil Balmond, with Arup
Photograph © Sylvain Deleu

Serpentine Pavilion 2003,
designed by Oscar Niemeyer
Photograph © Sylvain Deleu

Serpentine Pavilion 2005, designed by
Álvaro Siza and Eduardo Souto de Moura
with Cecil Balmond – Arup
Photograph © Sylvain Deleu

Serpentine Pavilion 2006,
designed by Rem Koolhaas
and Cecil Balmond, with Arup
Photograph © John Offenbach

Serpentine Pavilion 2007,
designed by Olafur Eliasson & Kjetil Thorsen
Photograph © Luke Hayes

*Lilas*: an installation by Zaha Hadid Architects,
Zaha Hadid and Patrik Schumacher, 2007
Photograph © Luke Hayes

Serpentine Pavilion 2008,
designed by Frank Gehry
Photograph © John Offenbach

Serpentine Pavilion 2009,
designed by Kazuyo Sejima
and Ryue Nishizawa of SANAA
Photograph © Nick Guttridge

Serpentine Pavilion 2010,
designed by Jean Nouvel
Photograph © Philippe Ruault

Serpentine Pavilion 2011,
designed by Peter Zumthor
with a garden by Piet Oudolf
Photograph © 2011 Walter Herfst

Serpentine Pavilion 2012, designed by
Herzog & de Meuron and Ai Weiwei
Photograph © 2012 Iwan Baan

Serpentine Pavilion 2013,
designed by Sou Fujimoto
Photograph © 2013 Iwan Baan

Serpentine Pavilion 2014,
designed by Smiljan Radić
Photograph © 2014 Iwan Baan

selgascano process book

pp.12–3
Model of Serpentine Pavilion 2015
Photograph © 2015 Iwan Baan

pp.14–5, top left p.16
Photographs © Adrian Ray

All other sketches, drawings, diagrams,
composite images and process photographs
of the Serpentine Pavilion 2015
© 2015 selgascano

Project Team
Serpentine Pavilion 2015

Architects

Lucía Cano and José Selgas
selgascano

Architectural Team

Bárbara Bardín
Julio Cano
Víctor Jiménez
María Levene
Elisabeth Molina
Antonio Mondéjar
Billy Morgan
Julián Ocampo
Inés Olavarrieta
Paolo Tringali
selgascano

Project Directors

Julia Peyton-Jones with Hans Ulrich Obrist
Serpentine Galleries

Project Leader

Julie Burnell
Serpentine Galleries

Project Curators

Emma Enderby and Jochen Volz
Serpentine Galleries

Engineering, Technical Design
and Cost Management

David Glover with
Thomas Webster
Michael Orr
Jack Wilshaw
Katja Leszczynska
AECOM

Consultants

Barnaby Collins and Katie Smith
DP9

Construction

Ted Featonby with Alan Doyle
Stage One Creative Services Ltd

Jeremy Singleton
The Technical Department Ltd

Project Advisors

Lord Palumbo, Chairman Emeritus
Serpentine Board of Trustees

Colin Buttery, Director of Parks
The Royal Parks

Andy Williams, Parks Superintendent
The Royal Parks

Ben Dalton and Kate Green
Planning Office,
Westminster City Council

Hassan Lashkariani
Building Control Officer,
Westminster City Council

Jenny Wilson, Licensing Officer,
Westminster City Council

London Fire and Emergency
Planning Authority

London Region, English Heritage

Friends of Hyde Park and
Kensington Gardens

## Serpentine Galleries Staff List

Director, Serpentine Galleries and Co-Director, Exhibitions and Programmes
Julia Peyton-Jones

Co-Director, Exhibitions and Programmes and Director of International Projects
Hans Ulrich Obrist

### Operations

Chief Operating Officer
Ian Dixon

Operations and Planning Officer
Roxanne Tahbaz

### Executive Support

Executive Assistant to Julia Peyton-Jones
Laura May Lewis

Personal Assistant to Julia Peyton-Jones
Claire Richards

Executive Assistant to Hans Ulrich Obrist
Laura Macfarlane

Personal Assistant to Hans Ulrich Obrist
Emily Purser

### Programmes

Head of Programmes
Jochen Volz

Gallery Manager
Mike Gaughan

Production and Installation Manager
Joel Bunn

Exhibitions Curator
Emma Enderby

Exhibitions Curator
Amira Gad

Exhibitions Curator
Rebecca Lewin

Assistant Curator
Melissa Blanchflower

Assistant Curator
Agnes Gryczkowska

Curator, Public Programmes
Lucia Pietroiusti

Assistant Curator, Public Programmes
Claude Adjil

Projects Curator
Amal Khalaf

Education Curator
Alex Thorp

Education Assistant Curator
Emily Rand

Education Assistant Curator
Ben Messih

Curator of Digital
Ben Vickers

### Communications

Head of Communications
Rose Dempsey

Head of Media Relations
Miles Evans

Communications Print Manager
Mary Lehner

Media and Communications Officer
V Ramful

Communications Assistant
Poppy Cockburn

Senior Digital Producer
Rosie Cardiff

Digital Content Editor (Interim)
Honour Bayes

### Development & Events

Head of Development
Faith Griffiths

Head of Development (Interim)
Laura Palmer

Head of Operations (Development)
Laura Halstead

Head of Individual Giving
Lucy Robertson

Head of Individual Giving
Ian Vallance (Interim)

Individual Giving Manager
Bethany Childs

Membership Manager, Individual Giving
Rachel Stephens

Development Executive
Mary Brooke Dreux

Head of Grants, Trusts & Foundations
Emma Claridge

Senior Trusts and Foundations Coordinator
Sarah Hardie

Corporate Membership Manager
Flora Goodwin

Development Consultant
Gillian Anderson Price

Data Coordinator
Bryony Dutta

Development Administrator
Kelsey Shave

Head of Events
Jelena Panza

Senior Events Manager
Juliette McCrimmon

Events Assistant
Betty Khiavi

Finance

Head of Finance
Graham Clark

Finance Consultant
Jonathan Smith

Senior Finance Officer
Barbara Stylska

Human Resources

Human Resources Manager (Interim)
Caroline Cromarty

Human Resources Assistant
Robertta Marques dos Santos

Projects

Head of Projects and Buildings
Julie Burnell

Facilities

Facilities Manager
Shahrul Amin

Facilities Assistant
Lucky Anthony

Facilities Assistant
Roderick Taylor

Limited Editions

Commercial Manager
Tom Harrisson

Editions Assistant
Matthew Johnstone

Archivist
Clare Colvin

Visitor Services

Head of Visitor Services (Interim)
Lisa Bullock

Visitor Services Manager (Interim)
Joy Middlebrook

Visitor Service Manager
Brittany Høie

Visitor Service Team Leaders
Chris Bayley
Mike Ditchburn
Jamie Fitzpatrick
Seamus Gough

Visitor Services Sales Assistant
Sophie Blagden
Eve Carson
Beth Fox
Laoise Meek
Kate Turner

Gallery Assistants
Dee Akhtar
Chris Alton
Anna Artale
Ashleigh Austin
Gonçalo Birra
Nathan Bowen
Ellie Bradford
Phoebe Bradford
Gareth Cadwallader
William Carter
Lucia Cherata
Dwayne Coleman
Catriona Collins
Rose De Lara
Hannah Edward
Chantel Forrester
Christina Friis
Michael Green
Samantha Harvey
Daniel Hatton
Lily Hawkes
Holly Hendry
Rachel Hill
Suzy Lawlor
Erica Lindberg
Owain McGilvary
Katherine Midgley
George Morris
Sophie Northcott
Laura Rouzet
Jacintha Thomas
Debii White
Yan White
Roger (Rojazad) Zorlu

The Serpentine Galleries thanks the many individuals, trusts, foundations and companies whose generosity and foresight enables people of all ages to engage with internationally renowned contemporary Exhibitions, Architecture, Design, Education and Public Programmes. Their support is vital to the ongoing success of the Serpentine Galleries.



Serpentine Sackler Gallery Founders

The Dr. Mortimer and Theresa
Sackler Foundation
Ilene Sackler Lefcourt
Kathe A. Sackler M.D.
Samantha S. Sackler Hunt.
Mortimer D.A. Sackler
Marissa T. Sackler
Sophia D. Sackler Dalrymple
Michael D. Sackler

Serpentine Sackler Gallery Founding Patrons

Bloomberg Philanthropies
LUMA Foundation
The David Ross Foundation
Lars Windhorst
Tatiana Taypina
The Wolfson Foundation

Serpentine Sackler Gallery
Founding Benefactors

Jenifer Evans
Nicoletta Fiorucci
J. Paul Getty Jnr. Charitable Trust
Stephen and Yana Peel
Catherine Petitgas
Sir Spas and Lady Roussev

Serpentine Sackler Gallery
Founding Artist Patrons

Ron Arad
Richard Artschwager
John Baldessari
Phyllida Barlow
Matthew Barney
Louise Bourgeois
Cecily Brown
Glenn Brown
Anthony Caro
John Currin
Thomas Demand
Olafur Eliasson
Fischli/Weiss
Yang Fudong
Gilbert & George
Felix Gonzalez-Torres
Douglas Gordon
Antony Gormley
Subodh Gupta
Andreas Gursky
N.S. Harsha
Susan Hefuna
Damien Hirst
M.F. Husain
Jitish Kallat
Anish Kapoor
Ellsworth Kelly
Bharti Kher
Karen Kilimnik
Jeff Koons
Yayoi Kusama
Maria Lassnig
Annie Leibovitz
Takashi Murakami
Shirin Neshat
Chris Ofili
Gabriel Orozco
Richard Prince
Paula Rego
Gerhard Richter
Ed Ruscha
Cindy Sherman
Hiroshi Sugimoto
Do-Ho Suh
Wolfgang Tillmans
Rirkrit Tiravanija
Rebecca Warren
Gillian Wearing
Rachel Whiteread
Richard Hamilton (Education)

Serpentine Gallery 40th Anniversary
Founding Benefactors

Jeanne and William Callanan
The Highmont Foundation
LUMA Foundation

And Founding Benefactors who
wish to remain anonymous.

Council of the Serpentine Galleries

Rob Hersov *Chairman*
Tatiana Akhmedova
Igor and Natasha Akhmerov
Mr and Mrs Kamel Alzarka

Nicolas Berggruen
Dorothy Berwin and Dominique Levy
Blavatnik Family Foundation
Natalia Bondarenko
Jeanne and William Callanan
Michael and Erin Cohen
Penny Coulter
Dag Cramér
Aud and Paolo Cuniberti
Zeynep Dereli
Griet Dupont
Jenifer Evans
Nicoletta Fiorucci and Giovanni Russo
Wendy Fisher
Tim Franks and Andrew Pirrie
Cecilie and Kathrine Fredriksen
Sasan and Yassmin Ghandehari
Marian Goodman
Mr and Mrs Lorenzo Grabau
Richard and Odile Grogan
David Harding
Susan and Richard Hayden
Helene and Johannes Huth
Mr and Mrs Tim Jefferies
Marie-Josée and Henry Kravis
LUMA Foundation
Nicole and Jean-Claude Marian
Svetlana Marich
Frédéric de Mevius
Jackie and Carl Michaelsen
Usha and Lakshmi N. Mittal
Sybil and Matthew Orr
Hideyuki Osawa, Boenfukyukai Foundation
Catherine and Franck Petitgas
The Don Quixote Foundation
Hans K Rausing
Julia Rausing
The Red Mansion Foundation
Nataliya Resh
Frances Reynolds
Yvonne Rieber
Charlotte Dauphin de La Rochefoucauld, Comtesse Charles-Henri de La Rochefoucauld
Galerie Thaddaeus Ropac
Sir Spas and Lady Roussev
Faraj Saghri
Robin Saunders
Anders and Yukiko Schroeder
Robin Scott-Lawson
David and Simone Sproul
Mr and Mrs Jerome Stern
Dayana Tamendarova
Tatiana Taypina
Serge Tiroche
Ted Vassilev
Robert and Felicity Waley-Cohen
Lars Windhorst
Manuela and Iwan Wirth

And members of the Council who wish to remain anonymous.

Council Circle of the Serpentine Galleries

Marlon Abela
Mrs Basil Al-Rahim
Sheikha Paula Al-Sabah
Mr and Mrs Harry Blain
Mark and Lauren Booth
Nicholas Candy
Carolyn Dailey
Russ Deleon
Marie Douglas
Denise Esfandi
Lawton W. Fitt and James I. McLaren Foundation
Yakir and Elena Gabay
Ingvild and Stephan Goetz
Olivier de Givenchy
Jonathan Goodwin
David Grob and Louise Hunt
Jennifer and Matthew Harris
Alison Jacques & Michael Conway
Kristi Jernigan
Ella Krasner
Matthew Mellon, in memory of Isabella Blow
Dalip and Chandrika Pathak
Eva Rausing
Mrs Nadja Swarovski-Adams
Ahmed and Cherine Tayeb
Robert Tomei
Andrei and Veronika Tretyakov
Andrew and Victoria Watkins-Ball
Michael and Anna Zaoui

And members of the Council Circle who wish to remain anonymous.

Americas Foundation of the Serpentine Galleries

Marina Abramović
Sarah Arison
Allison and Larry Berg
Laura and Lloyd Blankfein
Suzanne Deal Booth
The Broad Art Foundation
Daniel and Estrellita Brodsky
Debrina and Alessandro Cajrati Crivelli
Kathryn and Kenneth Chenault
Marco Compagnoni
Nancy and Steve Crown
Jennie L. and Richard K. DeScherer
The Diller - von Furstenberg Family Foundation
Trisha Donnelly
Jamie Drake
Linda and Gregory Fischbach
Jay Franke and David Herro
Leslie Fritz, Schiff Fine Art
Amanda and Glenn Fuhrman
Alexandra Garrison
Lauren Schor Geller and Martin Geller
Laurie and Peter Grauer
Agnes Gund

Marlene Hess and James D. Zirin
Kayne Foundation, Suzanne and Ric Kayne
Thomas L. and Katheryn P. Kempner
Marie-Josée and Henry Kravis
Leonard A. Lauder
Irina Liner
J. Jeffry and Elizabeth S. Louis Foundation
Catie and Donald Marron
Becky and Jimmy Mayer
Susan and Preston McSwain
Akiko Mikumo
Sandra and Stephen Muss
H. Tony and Marti Oppenheimer
Ronald O. Perelman
Maureen White and Steven Rattner
The Edward John and Patricia Rosenwald Foundation
The Dr. Mortimer and Theresa Sackler Foundation
Robin Saunders
Lisa Schiff, Schiff Fine Art
Douglas E. Schoen
John L. Silverman
The Paul E. Singer Foundation
Ed Skyler, Citi
Katherine Farley and Jerry Speyer
Gillian and Robert Steel
Rirkrit Tiravanija
Diane and Tom Tuft
Bradley Tusk and Dr Harper Montgomery
Ted Vassilev
Steven Volpe Design, Inc.
Patty Newburger and Brad Wechsler
Barbara and David Zalaznick

And members of the Americas Foundation of the Serpentine Galleries who wish to remain anonymous.

Founding Corporate Benefactor

Bloomberg

Platinum Corporate Benefactors

AECOM
Bloomberg
Coach
Goldman Sachs
Hiscox
J.P. Morgan Private Bank
My Beautiful City
Qatar Museums Authority
Weil, Gotshal & Manges

Gold Corporate Benefactors

COS
La Rinascente
Laurent-Perrier
The Space

Silver Corporate Benefactors

Chrome Hearts and Gareth Pugh
Eclipse
Grangewood
Phillips
Stage One

Bronze Corporate Benefactors

Davidson Kempner Capital Management LP
DLD Media GmbH
DP9
The Groucho Club
Peroni
Site Engineering Surveys Ltd (SES)
The Technical Department Ltd
Tellurian Capital Management LLP
Total Security Services
Veritas Event Services Ltd.
WEP
Zumtobel

Founding Corporate Members

American Express
Bloomberg
Citi
Foster + Partners
William Hare Group Limited

Annual Corporate Members

The Paul E. Singer Foundation

Serpentine Sackler Gallery Design Circle

Amina Technologies
Alias
Arabella Lennox-Boyd Landscape Design
Artemide
Burmatex
Dornbracht
Dyson Airblade
Elizabeth and Jeff Louis Foundation
Fenwick Elliott
Isometrix Lighting + Design
Pierre Lagrange and Roubi L'Roubi
Rise
Roca
Stage One
Stepevi
Whitco Catering Equipment Ltd

Education Projects supported by

Bloomberg

Education Programme supported by

Arts Council England
Marie Donnelly

David Fawkes and family
ForYourArt
Golden Bottle Trust
The Hayden Family Foundation
Marsh Christian Trust
Outset Contemporary Art Fund
Qatar Museums Authority
Qatar-UK 2013
The Sackler Trust
Andrei Tretyakov / Collectrium

And kind assistance from

The Royal Borough of Kensington and Chelsea

Exhibition Programme supported by

AECOM
Air de Paris, Paris
Shane Akeroyd
Anglo Chilean Society on behalf of the Alan Macdonald Endowment
artEDU Stiftung
Blondeau & Cie, Geneva
Bloomberg Philanthropies
Daniel Buren
Cabinet, London
Casey Kaplan, New York
Bilge & Haro Cumbusyan
Thomas Dane
Geyze Diniz
Lonti Ebers
Embassy of Argentina, London
Jay Franke and David Herro
Fundación Almine y Bernard Ruiz-Picasso para el Arte
Gagosian Gallery
Galeria Nara Roesler
Galerie Buchholz, Berlin/Cologne
Galerie Eva Presenhuber, Zürich
Galerie Krinzinger, Vienna
Galleria Continua
Goethe-Institut London
Goldman Sachs Gives – Lawton W. Fitt and James I. McLaren
Graham Foundation for Advanced Studies in the Fine Arts
Francis J. Greenburger
David Grob and Louise Hunt
Gumuchdjian Architects
Hauser & Wirth
The Henry Moore Foundation
Institut für Auslandsbeziehungen (ifa)
Isabella Bortolozzi Galerie
Jack Shainman Gallery, New York
Natascha Jakobs-Linssen, All Art Initiatives
John Kaldor and Naomi Milgrom Kaldor
Sean and Mary Kelly
Kunststiftung NRW
The Lars Windhorst Foundation
Lia Rumma Gallery Milano/Napoli
Lisson Gallery
LUMA Foundation
Ana and Marcelo Martins
Ulrich and Harriet Meyer
Usha and Lakshmi N. Mittal
Marina Nissim
Frances Reynolds
Ringier Collection, Zürich
Erica Roberts
Ruth and Richard Rogers
Marco and Luisa Rossi
Helen and Ken Rowe
Lynne Sable
Muriel & Freddy Salem
The Silvie Fleming Collection
Stanley Thomas Johnson Foundation
Julia Stoschek
Taka Ishii Gallery
Tanya Bonakdar Gallery, New York
Tatiana Taypina
Tellurian Capital Management LLP
Helen Thorpe
Trapiche
Ted Vassilev
White Cube

And those who wish to remain anonymous.

Learning Council: Committee

Jeanne and William Callanan
Gilberto Pozzi
Selina S. Sagayam

Learning Council

Catherine Lagrange
Mark and Elizabeth Thompson

Patrons

Marie-Claire, Baroness von Alvensleben
Seda Arbib
Makram Azar
Ron & Samantha Bauer
Colleen De Bonis
The Hon. Daniel Brennan
Richard and Basia Briggs
Friedrich B. Busse
Veronica Chou
Sir Ronald and Lady Cohen
Terence and Niki Cole
Alastair Cookson
Grace Contomichalos
Cynthia Corbett
Pilar Corrias
Davide Costa and Cristina Segni
Giulia Costantini
Bruce Eames and Sunday Riley Eames
Filatov Family Art Fund
The Edwin Fox Foundation
David Fawkes
Dima and Sabrina Friedman

Karine Giannamore
Francesca Guagnini
Nathalie Guiot, Thalie Art Foundation
G. Rustamova & J. Ahmadzada, Gyunel Ltd
Marc Hansen & Alessia Ciani
Mala and Oliver Haarmann
Sara Harrison
Eva and Iraj Ispahani
Anshu Jain, Co-Chief Executive Officer, Deutsche Bank AG
Mr and Mrs Karim Juma
Tessa Keswick
Mr and Mrs Simon Lee
May Noradee
Hussam Otaibi
Sayumi Otake
Christina Pamberg
Alexander Platon
Paul Price
Mr A.S. Rahman
Mr and Mrs Ivan Ritossa
Kimberley Robson
Scott Rudmann
Corinna zu Sayn-Wittgenstein
Finn Schouenborg Dombernowsky
Mr and Mrs Mark Shanker
Lt. Col. T S Spicer OBE
Caroline Stanbury
Per Skarstedt & Bona Montagu
Ian and Mercedes Stoutzker
Bruno Wang
Rebecca Wang
Welton Foundation
Paul Williams and Beth Stockley
Jonathan and Lucy Wood
Poju and Anita Zabludowicz

Future Contemporaries: Committee

HRH Princess Eugenie of York
Alia Al-Senussi
Magdalena Gabriel
Rebecca Guinness
Katherine Holmgren
Jemima Jones
Lucy McIntyre
Bobby Molavi
Jake Parkinson-Smith
Robin Scott-Lawson
Robert Sheffield
Andreas Siegfried
Christopher Taylor
Alexa Waley-Cohen
Michael Walker
Hikari Yokoyama

Future Contemporaries: Members

Noor Al-Rahim
Izabella Andersson, MBA
Marco Assetto
Alastair Balfour
Sarah-Louise Ballot-Lena and Steven Marcus
Anja and António Batista
Sarah Bourghardt
Mikael and Leonie Brantberg
Ben Bridgewater
Kate Bryan
Mary Charteris
Patrick C. Cunningham
Damian Delahunty
Sophie Demeyere
Flora Fairbairn
Federica Ferro Favero
Alessandra Mara de Freitas Ferrari
Valentina Fois
Nina Flohr
Leila Elizabeth Greiche
Marie Guerlain
Michael Hadjedj
Alexander Mason Hankin
Saïd Hejal
Matt Hermer
Henry Highley
Ceri Evan Hong-Tan
Kamel Jaber
Karim Jallad
Zoe Karafylakis Sperling
Daria Kirsanova
Bettina Korek
Christina Gee Kryca
Eva Lanskaya
Maged Latif
Clarisse Lehmann
James Lindon
Anna Lipskaya
Xi Liu and Yi Luo
Kitty Logsdail
Arianne Lovelace
Dan Lywood
Sonia Mak
Jean-David Malat
Ann-Marie Matthijs
Princess Alexandra Massimo di Roccasecca
John Paul Micalleff
Oliver Miro
Fernando J. Moncho Lobo
Zenouska Mowatt
Denis and Yulia Nagi
Isabelle Nowak and Torsten Winkler
Genie Oldenburg
Katharina Ottmann
Jake and Samira Parkinson-Smith
Joe Phelan
Mr R J Phillips
Carlos and Francesca Pinto
Maria-Theresia Pongracz
Lauren Prakke
Ruby Reed
Piotr Rejmer
Sibylle Rochat
Niklas Röhling
Chris Rust and Hillevi Gillanders

Valerie Sadoun
Poppy Sebire
Henrietta Shields
Edward and Charlotte Smallwood
Yassi Sohrabi
Irina Stark
Patricia Talalla
Edward Tang
Caroline Templeton
Anne-Marie Tong
Sydney Townsend and Mark Batup
Katie Trueman
Monuhar Ullah
Rachel Verghis
Marcus Waley-Cohen
Sam Waley-Cohen
Celia Weinstock
Bill and Anda Winters
Mr and Mrs Nabil Zaouk
Fabrizio D. Zappaterra
Loulua S. Zawawi
Alma Zevi

Benefactors

Jennifer and Skardon Baker
Anne Best and Roddy Kinkead Weekes
Marcus Boyle
Mervyn and Helen Bradlow
Geraldine Brodie
Benjamin Brown
Mrs Tita Granda Byrne
Lavinia Calza Beveridge
John Cavanagh
Sadie Coles
Carole and Neville Conrad
Monica and Knut Dahl
Count and Countess Hako von Finckenstein
David and Jane Fletcher
Jane and Richard Found
Eric and Louise Franck
Julie Gatland
David Gill
Dimitri J. Goulandris
Judith and Richard Greer
Jeremy Hargreave
Ren and Spencer Harman
Susan Harris
Maria and Stratis Hatzistefanis
Marianne Holtermann
Mrs Christine Johnston
Mr & Mrs C D Kapp
James and Clare Kirkman
Geraldine Larkin
Anne and Sydney Levinson
George and Angie Loudon
Andrew and Jacqueline Martin
Cary J. Martin
Penny Mather
Ruth and Robert Maxted
Viviane and James Mayor
Jeremy and Louisa Mobbs
Robin Monotti Graziadei
Dr Maigaelle Moulene
Mr and Mrs Paul Munford
Desmond Page and Asun Gelardin
Maureen Paley
Mrs Janaki Prosdocimi
Bruce and Shadi Ritchie
Jacqueline and Nicholas Roe
James Roundell
Ralph Segreti
Kaveh and Cora Sheibani
Kristy Stubbs
Simone and Robert Suss
Britt Tidelius
Audrey Wallrock
Alannah Weston
Helen Ytuarte White
Dr Yvonne Winkler
Henry and Rachel Wyndham
Mr and Mrs Nabil Zaouk
Jean-David Zorbibe

And Learning Council, Patrons, Future Contemporaries and Benefactors who wish to remain anonymous.

Public Funding by

Arts Council England

Serpentine Galleries summer season supported by

The Lars Windhorst Foundation

Serpentine Pavilion sponsored by

Goldman Sachs

Advisor

AECOM
with David Glover

Supported by Stage One

Gold Sponsor

Weil

Silver Sponsor

Grangewood

Bronze Sponsors

DavidsonKempner

DP9

Graham Foundation

PERONI ITALY

SES

the technical department

totalsecurity.co.uk

wep HSE

Patrons

Gumuchdjian Architects
Thomas Dane
And those who wish to remain anonymous

Serpentine Galleries supported by

LOTTERY FUNDED

Supported using public funding by ARTS COUNCIL ENGLAND

This catalogue is published to accompany the Serpentine Pavilion 2015 designed by selgascano, 25 June – 18 October 2015.

Editors: Emma Enderby and Jochen Volz
with thanks to Melissa Blanchflower and Melissa Larner
Spanish to English, interview translation: Robertta Marques dos Santos
Design: Fraser Muggeridge studio
Print: Lösch MedienManufaktur GmbH & Co. KG, Germany

First published by Koenig Books, London and the Serpentine Galleries, London.



ISBN 978-1-908617-27-9
(Serpentine Galleries, London)

ISBN 978-3-86335-793-1
(Koenig Books, London)



SERPENTINE GALLERIES

Serpentine Gallery
Kensington Gardens
London W2 3XA

Serpentine Sackler Gallery
West Carriage Drive
Kensington Gardens
London W2 2AR
Tel + 44 (0)20 7402 6075
Fax + 44 (0)20 7402 4103
www.serpentinegalleries.org

Koenig Books Ltd
At the Serpentine Gallery
Kensington Gardens
London W2 3XA
www.koenigbooks.co.uk

Distribution:

Germany & Europe
Buchhandlung Walther König
Ehrenstr. 4, 50672 Köln
Tel + 49 (0) 221 / 20 59 6-53
Fax + 49 (0) 221 / 20 59 6-60
verlag@buchhandlung-waltherkoenig.de

UK & Ireland
Cornerhouse Publications
70 Oxford Street
Manchester M1 5NH
Fon + 44 (0) 161 200 15 03
Fax + 44 (0) 161 200 15 04
publications@cornerhouse.org

Outside Europe
D.A.P. / Distributed Art Publishers, Inc.
155 6th Avenue, 2nd Floor
New York, NY 10013
Fon + 1 (0) 212 627 1999
Fax + 1 (0) 212 627 9484
eleshowitz@dapinc.com